Looking Back

A Photo Retrospective of the Mohawk Valley ~ Volume I

presented by

THE OBSERVER-DISPATCH
uticaOD.com

Acknowledgments

Every day, the *Observer-Dispatch* has the privilege of chronicling the lives of the wonderful people living in the Mohawk Valley. We revel in the opportunity to tell the many stories of accomplishment of the people, businesses and institutions of the communities we serve. And we try to be always mindful of the rich history of this region – a colorful tapestry woven of cultures and values and faith and hard work.

It is our pleasure to provide this unique pictorial perspective of the Mohawk Valley. We are very thankful for the assistance of the Oneida County Historical Society in compiling these wonderful photos, and for the talent and professionalism of many *Observer-Dispatch* staffers and associates, whose commitment helped bring this project to reality.

We hope you enjoy reading *"Looking Back: A Photo Retrospective of the Mohawk Valley"* as much as we enjoyed compiling it.

Donna M. Donovan
President and Publisher
The Observer-Dispatch

Published by Pediment Publishing, a division of The Pediment Group, Inc. www.pediment.com Printed in Canada

Table of Contents

Foreword

The Mohawk Valley Region has been marked by great change through the years – from the mid-1780s when veterans of the Revolutionary War and other Yankees from New England first began to settle here to the late 1950s when the area put the finishing touches on a monumental industrial revolution that was labeled "loom-to-boom era."

This beautiful section of Upstate New York was home to Native Americans for centuries. Permanent settlers began to arrive in the late 18th century and transformed the village of Utica into a transportation center to accommodate westbound pioneers. At the same time, the communities in the vicinity of Utica were dotted with dozens of farms and textile mills because creeks nearby were flowing fast enough at the time to turn the wheels of industry.

Those industries through the years – together with a variety of many other manufacturers – attracted immigrants. In the early 19th century, those immigrants came from northern and western Europe. Later in the century, they came from eastern and southern Europe. After World War II ended in 1945, the region attracted African-Americans, Hispanics and Asians.

This pictorial history celebrates the lives of the people who helped to shape the Mohawk Valley region during its first 175 years. The photos show them at work in schools and shops, in factories and on railroads and canals. It shows public officials at work and the region's residents at play, enjoying parades and celebrations and in their homes. And, it also shows some of the area's notable disasters, from destructive floods to train wrecks to fires.

The photos come from the Oneida County Historical Society's vast collection and also the archives of the *Observer-Dispatch*.

We hope you enjoy the trip down memory lane as it zigzags up and down the Mohawk Valley region.

CHAPTER ONE

Views of the Mohawk Valley

The Ice Age cometh about 10,000 years ago and its powerful sheets of ice – like a mighty farm plow – moved slowly south through New York State creating peaks and valleys, including the Mohawk Valley.

Then, those ice sheets retreated north and again left in their wake many famed places we know such as the Boonville Gorge, Trenton Gorge, the Tug Hill Plateau and the valleys Sauquoit and Oriskany.

Photographers through the years have taken wonderful photos of these and many similar places in the region – including bird's eye views via aerial shots in addition to photos of landscapes, cityscapes, hills and highways.

For centuries – up to the late 18th century – the Mohawk Valley Region had no permanent settlers or settlements, only thousands of acres of fertile soil, millions of tall stately trees and waterways galore – the mighty Mohawk River and creeks such as Sauquoit and Oriskany.

Then, in the mid-1780s came the first pioneers who dotted the landscape with houses, barns and fields of corn, squash and pumpkin.

That landscape changed dramatically in the first half of the 19th century when the Erie Canal and the Utica & Schenectady and the Utica & Syracuse Railroads appeared on the scene.

The landscape continued to change through the years as office buildings and factories went up and, in the 20th century, the automobile hit the road. Those roads were narrow and bumpy in the beginning, but as the century moved on, there appeared wide highways and arterials and, of course, the Thomas E. Dewey Thruway that passes through the region.

Left: View of Genesee Street, Utica, early 1900s. *Courtesy Oneida County Historical Society*

Right: Boonville Gorge with Black Canal lock and boat basin in foreground. *Courtesy Oneida County Historical Society*

Above: The Erie Canal in Utica, circa 1880, looking east from Washington Street toward Genesee Street. It is now Oriskany Blvd. *Courtesy Oneida County Historical Society*

Above: The Mohawk at Utica, early 1800s. *Courtesy Oneida County Historical Society*

Right: Washington and Genesee Streets, Utica, 1838. On the left is Washington Street with the First Presbyterian Church. *Courtesy Oneida County Historical Society*

Above: Main Street, looking north, Waterville, circa, 1871. *Courtesy Oneida County Historical Society*

Above: View of Trenton Falls, 1863. In the photo: Wm. H. Seward, Secretary of State; Baron DeStoecrel, Russian Minister; M. Molena, Nicaraguan Minister; Lord Lyons, British Minister; M. Mercier, French Minister; M. Schleiden, Hanseatic Minister; M. Bertenatti, Italian Minister; Count Piper, Swedish Minister; M. Bodisco, Secretary Russian Legation; Mr. Sheffield, Attaché British Minister; Mr. Donaldson, Mess. State Dept. U.S.A. *Courtesy Oneida County Historical Society*

Right: A view of downtown Utica in 1864, looking south along Genesee Street from the Busy Corner. *Courtesy Oneida County Historical Society*

Far left: Trenton Falls Gorge through which the West Canada Creek makes a spectacular fall over a three mile route. *Courtesy Oneida County Historical Society*

Left: Upper Gorge of West Canada Creek leading to Trenton Falls. *Courtesy Oneida County Historical Society*

Below: Bradish Block and Parker Building, east side of Genesee Street between Elizabeth and Bleecker streets, Utica, 1879. *Courtesy Oneida County Historical Society*

Above: The Erie Canal in the 1880s, passing by Washington Street in Utica, looking east toward Genesee Street. *Courtesy The Observer-Dispatch archives*

Left: A view of Genesee Street looking south over the Erie Canal Bridge (now Oriskany Street) toward Busy Corner in 1880. *Courtesy Oneida County Historical Society*

Below: Franklin Square, circa 1890. *Courtesy Oneida County Historical Society*

Above: Busy corner of Genesee Street looking north, circa 1890. *Courtesy Oneida County Historical Society*

Left: Main Street at Buell Avenue, looking west, circa 1890. *Courtesy Oneida County Historical Society*

Position: View of Sauquoit Creek, New York Mills, late 1800s. *Courtesy Oneida County Historical Society*

Above: Devereux Block, Genesee Street, Utica, circa 1890. *Courtesy Oneida County Historical Society*

Right: The Erie Canal looking west toward Genesee Street Bridge from John Street, circa 1895. *Courtesy The Observer-Dispatch archives*

Above: Forestport Break, September 18, 1899. *Courtesy Oneida County Historical Society*

Below: View of Little Falls, early 1900s. Notice the horse drawn buggy going over the bridge. *Courtesy Oneida County Historical Society*

Above: The Erie Canal in Ilion, circa 1900. *Courtesy The Observer-Dispatch archives*

Left: The Busy Corner, Bleecker and Genesee Streets in Utica, circa 1900. *Courtesy Oneida County Historical Society*

Above: Main Street, Waterville, circa 1905. *Courtesy Oneida County Historical Society*

Left: View of Oriskany Falls from Liberty Hill, circa 1905. *Courtesy Oneida County Historical Society*

Above: Bleecker Street, Utica, 1905. *Courtesy Oneida County Historical Society*

Above: View of Oriskany Falls, circa 1910. *Courtesy Oneida County Historical Society*

Left: Main Street, Oriskany Falls, 1908. *Courtesy Oneida County Historical Society*

Above: Genesee Street, Utica, circa 1915. *Courtesy Oneida County Historical Society*

Right: South Street, Bridgewater, early 1900s. *Courtesy Oneida County Historical Society*

Above: A bird's eye view of Oriskany, circa 1910. *Courtesy Oneida Coun* *Historical Society*

Left: View of Utica, circa 1917. *Courtesy Oneida County Historical Society*

Below: The Busy Corner in Utica, looking west, circa 1915. *Courtesy Oneid* *County Historical Society*

Left: Genesee Street, Utica, 1939. *Courtesy Oneida County Historical Society*

Below: Black River Canal north of Rome, 1935. *Courtesy Oneida County Historical Society*

CHAPTER TWO

Transportation Brings Prosperity

Transporation was the region's first large industry.

Pioneers from New England in the late 18th and early 19th centuries often stopped in the village of Utica on their way to the western territories. Utica not only was on the Mohawk river, but the main road heading west started at Bagg's Square in Utica and proceeded south to New Hartford and then west.

The pioneers would stop in Utica overnight or longer to have wagons repaired, provide horses with new pairs of shoes and buy supplies for their journey.

So, there sprung up in Utica and neighboring communities many hotels, taverns, inns, wagon repair shops, blacksmith shops and dry goods and grocery stores.

Between 1819 and 1840, the region became the home of the Erie Canal and the Utica & Schenectady Railraod. That contributed to the rapid growth of population in the region.

Through the years, transportation played an important role in the growth and prosperity of the Mohawk Valley Region.

Utica and Rome became main stops on the New York Central Railroad and in 1914 the railroad built a million dollar passenger terminal in Utica which still stands. The city also became one of Central's largest freight transfer centers.

Lateral canals in the 19th century were important to the area's growth, too. The Black River Canal connected the Erie Canal in Rome with the North Country. The Chenango Canal connected the Erie and in Utica with the Susquehanna River in Binghamton.

In the early years of the 20th century, newfangled automobiles arrived and with them came a demand for better roads and highways.

Left: First trolley to travel from Utica to New York Mills, circa 1890. *Courtesy Oneida County Historical Society*

Right: Street car at Columbia Street at DL & W Railroad crossing, Utica, 1920s. *Courtesy Oneida County Historical Society*

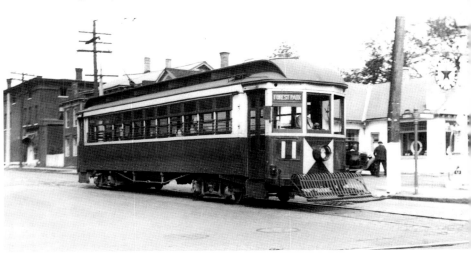

Right: Genesee Street horse-drawn trolley, late 1800s. *Courtesy Oneida County Historical Society*

Below: First trolley car to Whitesboro, 1890. *Courtesy Oneida County Historical Society*

Right: Empire State Express, circa 1891. Inaugurated by the New York Central & Hudson River Railroad Company, October 26, 1981 and was known as "The most famous train in the world." It went from New York to Buffalo, 440 miles in eight hours and 20 minutes with a stop in Utica. The fare was $9.25.
Courtesy Oneida County Historical Society

Above: Street cars in downtown Utica, late 1800s. *Courtesy Oneida County Historical Society*

Right: Stage coach in front of Bagg's Hotel, Utica, late 1800s. *Courtesy Oneida County Historical Society*

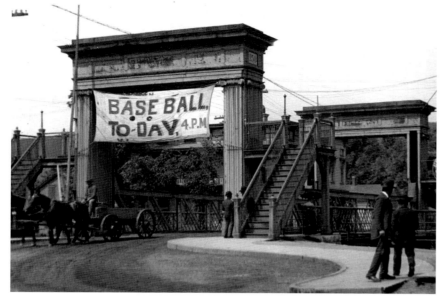

Left: Lift bridge across the Erie Canal in Ilion, late 1800s.
Courtesy Oneida County Historical Society

Right: Men work to pave Devereux Street in 1895. The view is from Genesee Street looking east toward Charlotte Street. Building on left is part of Butterfield House. Later the Roberts Company Dry Goods Store was there.
Courtesy Oneida County Historical Society

Below: Stagecoach to Canadarago Lake, late 1800s.
Courtesy Oneida County Historical Society

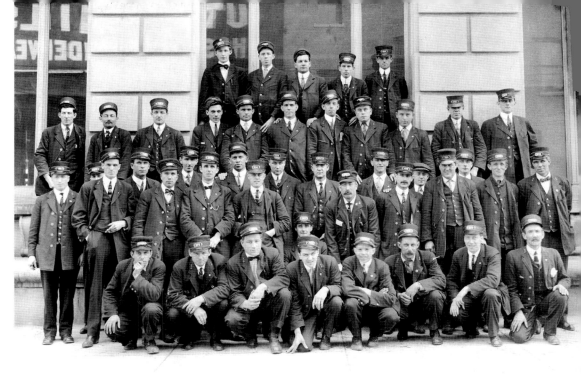

Above: Sylvan Beach train depot, circa 1900.
Courtesy Oneida County Historical Society

Above, right: Trolley operators, Utica, circa 1900.
Courtesy Oneida County Historical Society

Right: Train and employees at North Bookfield, 1900.
Courtesy Oneida County Historical Society

Above: DL&W train and staff at Richfield Springs, 1907. *Courtesy Oneida County Historical Society*

Opposite page: Utica women sit in a 1903 Winton in front of the Miller-Mundy Carriage Co. on Oneida Street in Utica. In the front seat are: Kate Baker, Roberts Sherman, and Clare Mundy Smith. In the back seat from left to right are: Alice Miller, Agnes Hyland, and a young boy named Henry Miller Jr. *Courtesy Oneida County Historical Society*

Right: Entrance to Summit Park, Oriskany, circa 1905. *Courtesy Oneida County Historical Society*

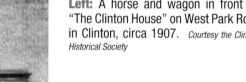

Above, left: Overhead crossing, Utica, circa 1910. *Courtesy Oneida County Historical Society*

Above, right: DL&W employees at Richfield Springs, circa 1907. *Courtesy Oneida County Historical Society*

Left: A horse and wagon in front of "The Clinton House" on West Park Row in Clinton, circa 1907. *Courtesy the Clinton Historical Society*

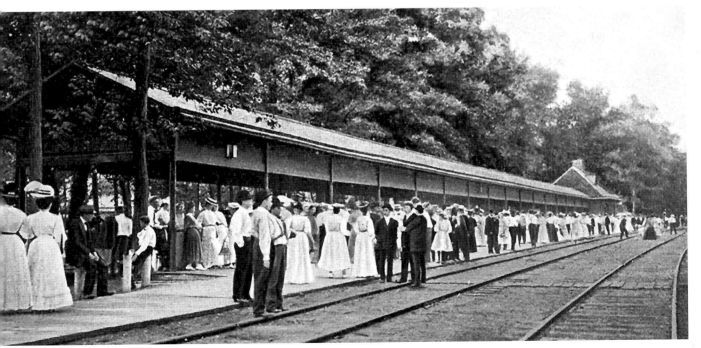

Above: Utica Electric Railway Tour. *Courtesy Oneida County Historical Society*

Left: Train station at Sylvan Beach, circa 1907. *Courtesy Oneida County Historical Society*

Above: DL&W train, F. Wilkie was the engineer. *Courtesy Oneida County Historical Society*

Above Right: Unidentified group waits for the train at the Forestport train depot, early 1900s. *Courtesy Oneida County Historical Society*

Right: Utica Richfield Express at Richfield Junction. *Courtesy Oneida County Historical Society*

Left & below: Eugene Godet demonstrates his flying machine over Utica during Utica Day festivities, September, 16, 1911. *Courtesy Oneida County Historical Society*

Bottom, left: The Hotel Utica Limo sits in front of the hotel on its opening night, March 12, 1912. The limo was used to pick up guests at the train depot on Main Street. *Courtesy Oneida County Historical Society*

Top, left and right: Construction of Union Station. *Courtesy Oneida County Historical Society*

Bottom Left: First west bound train No. 43 at new sub depot, 8:45 am, January 19, 1913. *Courtesy Oneida County Historical Society*

Bottom Right: Empire State Express in Utica, in the 1920's. *Courtesy Oneida County Historical Society*

Opposite page: Waterville train depot, circa 1915. *Courtesy Oneida County Historical Society*

CHAPTER THREE

Education Helps Shape the Region

Education has contributed significantly to the shaping of the Mohawk Valley Region. Schools dating back to the late 18th century and continuing through the 19th century were mostly white and male and trained some of the region's most prominent citizens. Among them: Ward Hunt, associate justice of the U.S. Supreme Court; Major General Daniel Butterfield, hero of the Civil War, and James Schoolcraft Sherman, vice president of the United States from 1909-12. Outstanding women of the time also trained in area schools, including Rose Cleveland, noted author, teacher and First Lady of the Land when her bachelor brother, Grover Cleveland, was elected president of the United States.

During late 19th and early 20th centuries, women and minorities began to attend area schools in large numbers.

The early schools were mostly private and parochial, but that later changed when the public school systems were established throughout the area.

Hamilton College was chartered in 1793, but it would take more than 150 years before other colleges appeared on the scene Utica College, Mohawk Valley Community College, SUNYIT and the Utica School of Commerce.

The region's hundreds of elementary and high schools have provided photographs through the years with hundreds of photo opportunities. Some of their work is shown here.

Left: The old Rome Free Academy, circa 1900. *Courtesy Oneida County Historical Society*

Right: The busy dining room at St. Vincent's Industrial School at Rutger Street and Conkling Avenue in East Utica. Photo was taken in the early 1900s. *Courtesy Oneida County Historical Society*

Above: Utica Free Academy students, 1897. *Courtesy Oneida County Historical Society*

Below: Whitestown Seminary students, circa 1874. *Courtesy Oneida County Historical Society*

Opposite page: Young Ladies' Seminary (Mrs. Piatt's School) at 726 Washington Street, Utica, late 1800s. *Courtesy Oneida County Historical Society*

Left: Dormitory at St. Vincent's Industrial School for Boys at Rutger Street and Conkling Avenue, circa 1880. *Courtesy Oneida County Historical Society*

Below, left: Whitestown Seminary, early 1900s. *Courtesy Oneida County Historical Society*

Below: Academy, Utica. *Courtesy Oneida County Historical Society*

Above: Utica Advanced School graduating class in the early 1900s, in front of the Courthouse in Utica. *Courtesy Oneida County Historical Society*

Left: Lincoln School, first grade students, circa 1900. Miss Florence Hicks was the teacher. Identified in the row by the window, starting at front: Alice Halligan, unidentified, Ella Henderson, Bessie Austin, Lilly Schwartz, Cornelia Andes, Ruth Roberts. The other students identified: Grover Lee, Leila Roberts, Mary Raymer, Agnes Mulhearny, Frances Fisher, Agnes Flanagan, Florence Scott, Anne Claes, Flora Andes and Helen Tesmer. *Courtesy Oneida County Historical Society*

Opposite page: Utica Free Academy following a fire in early 1900. *Courtesy Oneida County Historical Society*

Above: Bertha B. Smith Cecily Baker School students, 313 Court Street, Utica, early 1900s. *Courtesy Oneida County Historical Society*

Right: Miss Warner's School, Utica, circa 1900. *Courtesy Oneida County Historical Society*

Above: Hamilton Street School graduating class, Utica, 1902. *Courtesy Oneida County Historical Society*

Right: Hamilton College, Clinton, circa 1907. *Courtesy Oneida County Historical Society*

Looking Back

Left: Carnegie Hall, Hamilton College, Clinton, circa 1907. *Courtesy Oneida County Historical Society*

Below: James Kemble eighth grade graduation, 1908. *Courtesy Oneida County Historical Society*

Above: Francis Street School students, 1912. Students identified as: Howard Johnston, Leo Fisher, Edwin David, Franklin Steffen, William Kelly, Laverne Miller, John Clark, Earl Yeoman, Dorothy Reynolds, Edna Riley, Hazel Holman, Edna Bach, Margaret Pesch, Genevieve Murphy, Helen Allen, Jeannette Murphy, Josephine Chester, Alice Leard, Corrine Jones, Pearl Becraft, Hazel Wilburt, Magdalene Vogler, Ralph McGawley, Leo Meagher, Hamilton Peck. *Courtesy Oneida County Historical Society*

Above, right: Old Utica Academy on Bleeker Street. *Courtesy Oneida County Historical Society*

Right: Camden School students, circa 1908. *Courtesy Oneida County Historical Society*

Above, left: Deerfield High School. *Courtesy Oneida County Historical Society*

Above: Augusta School students pose for the photographer on Arbor Day, May 4, 1915. *Courtesy Oneida County Historical Society*

Left: Miller Street School children in Utica, circa 1918. *Courtesy Oneida County Historical Society*

Above: First Chadwicks High School graduation class, 1922. Back Row: Dorothy Emry, Anna Maloney, Mary McDonald, Vincent Murphy, Ruth Philio. Front Row: Principal a Stanton, Mildred Kuhn, Ethel Richards, History Teacher Miss Barrett. *Courtesy The bserver-Dispatch archives*

Opposite page: Boys attending St. Vincent's Industrial School in 1920. The school was located on Rutger Street and Conkling Avenue in East Utica. *Courtesy Oneida County Historical Society*

Above, right: Kemble School graduation, 1925. *Courtesy Oneida County Historical Society*

Below: Miss Van Marter's first grade class, Chadwicks School, mid 1930s. *Courtesy The bserver-Dispatch archives*

Below, right: St. Francis de Sales High School senior prom, 1939. *Courtesy Oneida County Historical Society*

Opposite page: Kemble School students, 1925. Kenneth S. Hurd is the only one identified with the clarinet. *Courtesy Oneida County Historical Society*

Left: Utica Catholic Academy. *Courtesy Oneida County Historical Society*

Above: Whitesboro Central School year book staff, 1938. Left to right, seated: Dorothy Lebejewski, John Cox, Robert Hauser, Marion Clark, Robert Williams, Philip Dumka, Beatrice Anderson. Standing, first row: Dorothy Casler, Doris Evans, Marion Hughes, Rose Guido, Phyllis White, Margaret Sterling, Dorothy Cox, Betty Wind, Helen Gifford, Betty Andrew, Jennie Wolak, Lucille La Shombe. Back row: George Besig, Thomas Mort, John Leach, Henry Wise. *Courtesy Oneida County Historical Society*

CHAPTER FOUR

Area Bustles With Commerce

The first settlers arrived in the Mohawk Valley Region in the mid-1780s and from the very beginning most of them cleared the forest and began to farm the land. A handful, however, opened businesses - from dry goods stores to wagon repair shops to general stores.

As the area grew in population, so did the number of stores and commercial enterprises.

Bagg's Hotel in Utica was one of the first commercial successes and by the mid 19th century the area was dotted with dozens of hotels, inns and taverns. Many of them were built to accommodate westbound travelers who would stop overnight in the region to rest and resupply before heading to western territories.

There also appeared in the area in those early days restaurants, blacksmith shops, jewelry stores, mineries, dressmaking shops, hardware stores, pottery works and cabinetmakers.

Many of the businesses were family-owned and employed not only husband and wife but also their children.

Banking also quickly became a major business and by the early 19th century there were dozens of banks in the area. Some were owned by local persons, while others were branches of larger banks in New York city.

Downtown Utica in the first half of the 20th century was the cultural, commercial and professional center of the region. It was the home of many first-run theaters restaurants, department stores and five-and-dimes. In the 1870s, Frank W. Woolworth opened his first five-cent store on Bleecker Street in Utica. It evolved into the vast chain that dominated the country for years.

Left: West side of Genesee St. between Columbia and Lafayette taken in about 1870. *Courtesy Oneida County Historical Society*

Right: John Roberts Department Store in downtown Utica on Genesee Street, circa 1900. *Courtesy Oneida County Historical Society*

Above left: Variety Store, Washington Mills, 1884. Included in the photo: Al Davis, Fred Clark, W.H. Davis, George Clark, Wm. Scovill, Wallace Chapman, Mr. Gardner. *Courtesy Oneida County Historical Society*

Above: City T Store on the 100 block of Bleecker Street. Utica, late 1800s. *Courtesy Oneida County Historical Society*

Left: Bagg's Hotel in Utica as it appeared sometime between 1865-1869. *Courtesy Oneida County Historical Society*

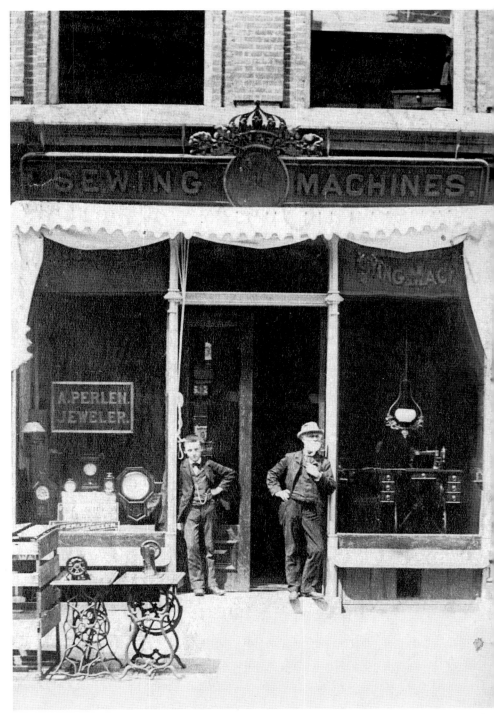

Above: Barbers in the Butterfield House Barber Shop at Genesee and Devereux streets in Utica, circa 1903. *Courtesy Oneida County Historical Society*

Right: A. Perlen Jeweler, 109 Bleecker Street, Utica, 1887. *Courtesy Oneida County Historical Society*

Below: The Park House Hotel was built at the northern end of the Village Park in Clinton in the summer of 1800, and for a number of years was the only hotel in the village. *Courtesy Oneida County Historical Society*

Above: P.F. Scheidelman, dealer in butter, cheese and eggs, early 1900s. It was located at 521 Varick Street, Utica. *Courtesy Oneida County Historical Society*

Right: City National Bank building, Utica, circa 1905. *Courtesy Oneida County Historical Society*

Below: Fraser's Muslin underwear and corset department, Utica, circa, 1910. *Courtesy Oneida County Historical Society*

Above left: Kohlers dry goods on Varick Street, Utica, early 1900s. It later became Kohlers Restaurant. *Courtesy Oneida County Historical Society*

Above: Francis Miller, center, and Harry Mundy, Utica's first car dealers, sit in a new Winton in front of their garage on Oneida Square in 1903. *Courtesy Oneida County Historical Society*

Left: Singer Sewing machine display at the Old Butterfield House on Genesee Street, Utica, December, 1890. *Courtesy Oneida County Historical Society*

Opposite page: Utica Motor Car Company on Bleecker Street, across from Chancellor Park, circa 1906. Behind the wheel of the 1906 Pierce Arrow is Tony Ledermann, one of the top mechanics in the area and the man in charge of Utica Motor Car Company's repair department. Ledermann later opened a Pierce-Arrow dealership at Plant and Hart streets in Utica. *Courtesy Oneida County Historical Society*

Left: Utica Motor Car Co., 333-337 Bleecker Street, Utica, circa 1907. A 1907 Buick is first in line. *Courtesy Oneida County Historical Society*

Below: Utica Motor Car Co., 333-337 Bleecker Street, Utica, circa 1906. *Courtesy Oneida County Historical Society*

Above: Herman P. Klube and Albert W. Germann in the drapery department of Robert Fraser's old store on Genesee Street, Utica, circa 1906. *Courtesy Oneida County Historical Society*

Right: Butterfield House, Utica, circa 1905. *Courtesy Oneida County Historical Society*

Below: Office and salesroom of Roberts Hardware Co., Utica, 1910. *Courtesy Oneida County Historical Society*

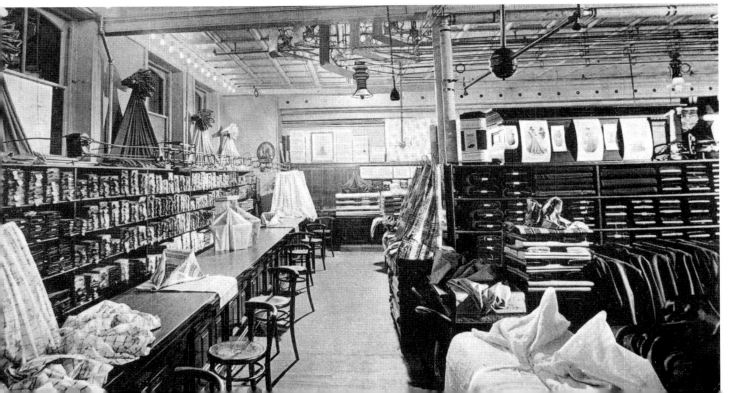

Above: John A. Roberts & Co., silk department, 1910. It was located at 169-171 Genesee Street, Utica. *Courtesy Oneida County Historical Society*

Left: John A. Roberts & Co., black and colored dress goods department, 1910.

Courtesy Oneida County Historical Society

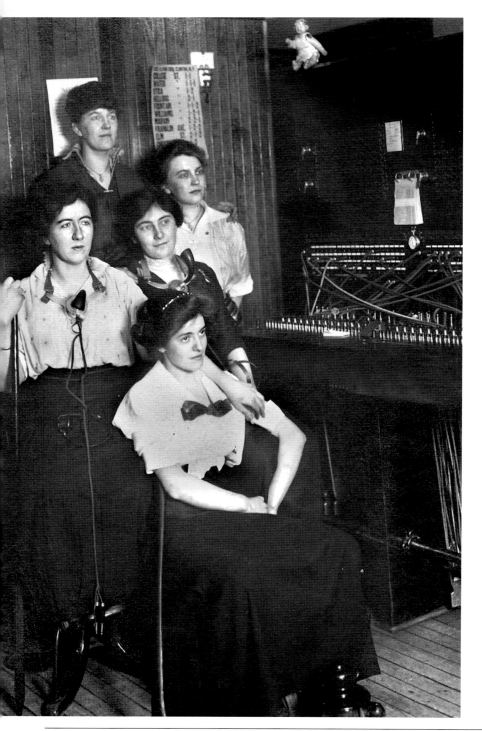

Left: First Telephone office in Clinton in the early 1900s. It was located on Williams Street. Photo shows type of switchboard then in use. Cart on wall indicates method of fire alarm signals. On extreme left is Miss Agnes Duffy. *Courtesy the Clinton Historical Society*

Right: G.W. Payne, jeweler and optician at 178 Genesee Street, Utica, circa, 1910. *Courtesy Oneida County Historical Society*

Below: Schultz's fancy baked goods and grocery delivery wagon powered by a Harley Davidson motorcycle, circa 1915. *Courtesy Oneida County Historical Society*

Above: Employees of the Commercial Department, telephone company, 1911. *Courtesy Oneida County Historical Society*

Left: Hotel Martin on Bleecker Street, Utica, circa 1910. *Courtesy Oneida County Historical Society*

Below: Kresge's Corner, Utica, circa 1910. *Courtesy Oneida County Historical Society*

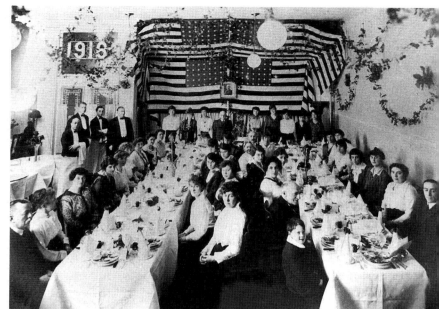

Above: Sullivan & Slawson's Drug Store at 158-160 Genesee Street, Utica, circa 1915. *Courtesy Oneida County Historical Society*

Above, right: Employees of Tompkins-Coopernail Department Store pose for a photo during a banquet at the Bagg's Hotel in 1916. *Courtesy The Observer-Dispatch archives*

Right: New York Telephone Co. employees and truck, circa 1917. *Courtesy Oneida County Historical Society*

Above: First National Bank lobby, Oriskany Falls, circa 1920. Left to right: Walter Terry, Elise Walter, Howard Staehla. *Courtesy Oneida County Historical Society*

Left: Hotel Utica, circa 1918. *Courtesy Oneida County Historical Society*

Left: Miller Electric Co., on Genesee Street, Utica, circa 1920. Grover Miller is on the left and his brother Clarence Miller on the right. *Courtesy Oneida County Historical Society*

Below, left: Arlington Food Market, hotel and Lippman's Clothes Shop at 182-184 West Dominick Street, Rome, 1920s. *Courtesy Oneida County Historical Society*

Below: Mr. Anthony Marraffa, butcher & grocer who ran a meat market at 300 Kossuth Avenue in Utica. The photo was taken in 1929. *Courtesy Oneida County Historical Society*

Above: Men pose in front of the National Bank of Clayville in 1926 as a double-door large safe was being delivered to the bank. The building was built in 1876 as a school and still stands today. *Courtesy the Town of Paris Historical Society*

Left: Fraser's Department Store's Roof Restaurant, 1925. *Courtesy Oneida County Historical Society*

Below: Utica Ice company employees and delivery trucks, circa 1930. *Courtesy Oneida County Historical Society*

Opposite page: Utica Gas & Electric company employees and truck, circa 1930s. *Courtesy Oneida County Historical Society*

Above: The Mayro Building on the southeast corner of Genesee and Bank Place, 1937. *Courtesy Oneida County Historical Society*

Above, right: Boston Store, Utica, early 1930s. *Courtesy Oneida County Historical Society*

Right: Maher Building, Utica, 1933. *Courtesy Oneida County Historical Society*

Below: Partners and brothers George, left, and Niem Jweid, right, pose for a photo outside of their South Street Store in the early 1930s. *Courtesy Oneida County Historical Society*

CHAPTER FIVE

Early Industry Fuels Rapid Growth

Industry played an important role in the rapid growth of the Mohawk Valley region.

Before 1850, the area was home to a variety of industries, from wagon-making to tool-making to soap-making. From 1850 to 1950, however, the major industry was the textile industry.

The region was home to hundreds of textile mills, big and small, making everything from knit underwear to sweaters to caps to ready-made dresses and suits.

Textile mills employed thousands of men and women and was responsible for attracting tens of thousands of immigrants to the area through the years. First came the Germans the late 1840s and early 1850s. Later in the century the mills provided work for immigrants from Poland and Italy.

But there was more to the area's industrial picture than textiles. Through the years hundreds of manufacturers settled in the area and gave employment to many. They made a great variety of goods, including beds and bed springs, heaters and air conditioners, washing machines, furniture, guns, copper and brass godds, silverware and sports equipment.

In the early 1900s, the area was on the verge of becoming an automoblie manufacturing center. The Remington and the Loco-mobile automobiles were made here as were automobile bodies by Willoughby and mufflers by Powell.

The region gained national fame in the 1950s after most its textile mills had moved south. Civic leaders and politicians worked together and put toether a plan to attract industries. Their plan worked.

During that "loom-to-boom" era, the region became the home of such manufacturers as General Electric, Chicago Pneumatic, Bendix Aviation, Sperry Univac and many others.

Left: Oneida County glacial soils provided accessible gravel, aggregate and stone in 1880 for road and canal construction crews. *Courtesy Oneida County Historical Society*

Right: Durhamville Dry Dock, Durhamville, late 1800s. *Courtesy Oneida County Historical Society*

Above: Old Grist Mill dam at Gravesville, early 1900s. *Courtesy Oneida County Historical Society*

Above Right: View of the old Dye-house at New York Mills. No. 3 and 4 Mills built as a grist or flour mill about the year 1800 by General George Doolittle of Whitestown, father-in-law of Benj. S. Walcott, father of W.D. Walcott. The mill was for many years the only flouring mill within 40 miles and was called the Burrstone Mill, from the stones used in grinding, being, the French Burr Mill-stones. This mill was changed and altered into a cotton factory by Benj. S. Walcott after his marriage to the General's daughter. Benj. S. Walcott transferred the care of the mill to his brother, Wm. Walcott and the mill's reputation as the manufacturer of superior cotton goods became known throughout the country. This mill was known as the first cotton factory west of the state of Rhode Island and was a stock company composed of Benj. S. Walcott, his son of the same name, the father and grandfather of W.D. Walcott. In this mill the first power loom was started so far as known in America and the cotton used was picked or prepared for carding by hand, sent out to families for that purpose previous to the invention of the picking machinery. *Courtesy Oneida County Historical Society*

Right: Clearing the land for Black River Canal, September 21, 1889. *Courtesy Oneida County Historical Society*

Opposite page: Clearing the land for Black River Canal, September 21, 1889. *Courtesy Oneida County Historical Society*

Above: Breinerd Farm, Canning Factory Road, Waterville, circa 1900. Driver is William Rhys Pugh. On wagon is Rev. Richard P. O'Connor. The boy is Leonard Wilson (son of Dr. Wilson of Waterville). Man on the ground is George Rowe. *Courtesy Oneida County Historical Society*

Opposite page: Clearing the land for Black River Canal, September 21, 1889. *Courtesy Oneida County Historical Society*

Right: The Erie Canal looking east flows by the Remington Arms and Ammunition plant in Ilion, circa 1900. *Courtesy The Observer-Dispatch archives*

Above: Globe Woolen Mills, Utica, circa 1905. *Courtesy Oneida County Historical Society*

Opposite page: Group of hop pickers at Paris Hill, 1900. *Courtesy Oneida County Historical Society*

Right: Olympian Knit Goods Co., New Hartford, circa 1905. *Courtesy Oneida County Historical Society*

Below: American Wood Board Co., Clark Mills, circa 1905. *Courtesy Oneida County Historical Society*

Above: Construction of the Barge Canal, Marcy, early 1900s. *Courtesy Oneida County Historical Society*

Left: Logging Camp, Verona Beach, 1908. *Courtesy Oneida County Historical Society*

Below, left: Interior of Rome machine shop. *Courtesy Oneida County Historical Society*

Below: Camden Knitting Co., Camden, circa 1910. *Courtesy Oneida County Historical Society*

Looking Back

Above: Construction of the Delta Dam and Black River Canal, early 1900s. *Courtesy Oneida County Historical Society*

Right: Albert Bohling poses in his shop, Bohling's Blacksmith Shop on Third Avenue, between Rutger and South streets, in East Utica, 1931. It was one of the last blacksmith shops in the city. *Courtesy Oneida County Historical Society*

Below: Work on the Barge Canal began in 1903 and the canal was opened in 1918. This photo was taken in 1910 and shows work being done in Frankfort. *Courtesy The Observer-Dispatch archives*

Above: West End Brewing Co., 1913. *Courtesy Oneida County Historical Society*

Above, left: A flag raising at the site of the New York Mills mills on May 19, 1917 drew a small crowd of mill workers and their families. *Courtesy New York Mills Historical Society*

Left: Employees of Rome Textile head for Sylvan Beach along the Erie Canal in Rome for an outing in the summer of 1922. *Courtesy Oneida County Historical Society*

Above: West End Brewing Co., 1913. *Courtesy Oneida County Historical Society*

Right: New York Mills, Juilliard Mill #2. *Courtesy Oneida County Historical Society*

Below: Workers in knitting room at the Paragon Knitting Mill in Utica in 1925. *Courtesy Jackie Knobloch*

Above: Workers from the Savage Arms Corporation on Turner Street, Utica, take a moment to pose for the photograph in 1927. *Courtesy Oneida County Historical Society*

Opposite page: Assembly room at Savage Arms in Utica, circa 1927. The company manufactured guns, washing machines and ice-cream cabinets. *Courtesy Oneida County Historical Society*

Looking Back

CHAPTER SIX

Culturally Diverse Society Emerges

As with most of the United States

at the turn of the 19th century, religion played a large role in everyday life for residents of the Mohawk Valley Region.

Due to the many different ethnic origins of those who came to settle in the area, churches and worship centers were organized mainly around the different cultural backgrounds of the residents.

In many cases, like that of the early Catholic and Protestant residents, congregations from different churches and ethnic groups aided one another to develop their own parishes. This often meant sharing churches and other buildings while also helping each other financially.

These burgeoning parishes soon amassed enough funds to create their own individual churches complete with splendid architecture. Many of the buildings, such as the Hamilton College Chapel in Clinton, showcased a level beauty and craftsmanship that warranted them to become popular images nationwide.

However, religious sites were not the only places for newly settled immigrants to meet and interact.

Countless clubs, organizations and eateries-such as the

Knights of Columbus and Kohler's Restaurant on Varick Street in Utica- sprang up around the Mohawk Valley Region that displayed the true diversity and splendor of its inhabitants.

Opposite: Oneida Community, circa 1866. *Courtesy Oneida County Historical Society*

Right: The Unitarian Church at Trenton, 1898. *Courtesy Oneida County Historical Society*

Right: Meeting of the Central New York Farmer's Club at the home of James V.H. Scovill, Paris, circa 1880. *Courtesy Oneida County Historical Society*

Below, left: Bleecker Street Baptist Church at 128-134 Bleecker Street, Utica, circa 1886. The church was organized March 21, 1839. D.G. Corey was the pastor for 45 years. *Courtesy Oneida County Historical Society*

Below, middle: Mount Vernon Presbyterian Church, Vernon, circa 1878. *Courtesy Oneida County Historical Society*

Below, right: First Methodist Episcopal church on Oxford Road, New Hartford, circa 1890. *Courtesy Oneida County Historical Society*

Above: Dinner party at the home of George Hartness, North Gage, 1894. Left to right: Judith Preston, Carrie M. Hartness, Mrs. Seymour Forbes, Flora Preston, Seymour Forbes, Adoni J. Hartness, George Hartness, Charles Preston. *Courtesy Oneida County Historical Society*

Right: Interior of the Unitarian Church at Trenton, 1898. *Courtesy Oneida County Historical Society*

Below Right: St. John's Roman Catholic Church, Utica. *Courtesy Oneida County Historical Society*

Below: Interior of St. John's Roman Catholic Church, Utica. *Courtesy Oneida County Historical Society*

Above: New Hartford Presbyterian Church, early 1900s. *Courtesy Oneida County Historical Society*

Above, right: Grace Church and Butterfield House, Utica, circa 1905. *Courtesy Oneida County Historical Society*

Right: St. Paul's Church, Paris Hill, ten miles south of Utica, circa 1900. *Courtesy Oneida County Historical Society*

Right: Fort Herkimer Church, 1927. *Courtesy Oneida County Historical Society*

Below, left: First Presbyterian Church at the corner of Columbia Street, Utica, circa 1905. *Courtesy Oneida County Historical Society*

Below, right: Hiram Lodge No. 18 F.A.M. members pose for the photo at the Masonic Temple, 1927. The lodge opened May 17, 1925. Identified, first row: Dorothy Brown, Charles Titus, unknown, Kenny Bush, Johnny Jackson, Mrs. Fletcher, Charlie Howard, Gussie Wilburn, Willis Brooks, James Warnwerk, Sr. Second row: Mr. Howard, Mrs. Estridge, unknown, unknown, unknown, Alice Waters, Mrs. Jackson, unknown, Idel Wilburn, Anna Wilburn, Doris Wilburn, Laura King, unknown, Lillian Lewis. Row three: Unknown, Mrs. Howard, Francis Titus, Charlotte Fletcher, unknown, unknown, unknown, Jennie M. Frank, James Hamlett, Sr., Buster Manlett, Alice Hamlett, Mr. & Mrs. Rippey. *Courtesy Oneida County Historical Society*

CHAPTER SEVEN

Early Homes Reflect Affluence

Mohawk Valley Region residents who produced photographs of their homes generally reflected their affluence and wealth.

The cost of purchasing a camera or hiring a photographer often was too high for most working class members of society. Thus, the homes whose pictures are on record at most historical societies are those of the upper middle class and well to do of the area.

Large, gorgeous farm houses in Italianate and colonial style colored the rural landscape of the area. Many of the area's prominent members, such as Horatio Seymour, Benjamin Walcott, Samuel Campbell and the Weaver family-who settled most of North Utica- maintained lush family estates of which many are still standing today.

Other palatial homes sprang up in the city of Utica, lining Genesee Street, the city's main artery of transportation. Even more grandi-

ose homes were built in the Rutger Park and Cornhill areas of the city.

Meanwhile, the city of Rome laid haven to such large dwellings as the Jervis Home on North Washington Street, which was originally used as a building for holding for army munitions.

Left: Park House, Whitesboro, 1894. The house was built by Mrs. Mary Eldridge Corbett and James Corbett during 1893 and 1894. *Courtesy Oneida County Historical Society*

Right: Homes along Genesee Street, circa 1905. *Courtesy Oneida County Historical Society*

Above: Dodge-Pratt-Northam house, 106 Schuyler Street, Boonville, circa 1878.
Courtesy Oneida County Historical Society

Opposite page: Cottage at Sylvan Beach, 1888. Only person identified is Esther Graham on the balcony at left. *Courtesy Oneida County Historical Society*

Below: Residence of John Butterfield on Genesee Street, Utica, 1883. The house was built circa 1860. *Courtesy Oneida County Historical Society*

Above: Mr. James F. Martin's Homestead at Yorkville, late 1800s. *Courtesy Oneida County Historical Society*

Above, right: Flora Preston and Carrie M. Hartness prepare a meal at the home of George Hartness, North Gage, December 1894. *Courtesy Oneida County Historical Society*

Right: Residence at 318 Genesee Street, Utica, early 1900s. *Courtesy Oneida County Historical Society*

Above: Bacon House, Taberg, circa 1905. *Courtesy Oneida County Historical Society*

Left: Seymour House, Deerfield. *Courtesy Oneida County Historical Society*

Below: Homes along Railroad Street, Taberg, circa 1905. *Courtesy Oneida County Historical Society*

Above: Home of Mr. David Johnson Millard, Clayville, circa 1900. The home was built in 1775. *Courtesy Oneida County Historical Society*

Left: Captain Lewis' home at 907 Kellogg Avenue, Utica, 1907. *Courtesy Oneida County Historical Society*

Below: Benjamin S. Walcott house, New York Mills. *Courtesy Oneida County Historical Society*

Left: Mansion House in Sherrill, 1930s.
Courtesy Oneida County Historical Society

Below Left: Residence at 711 Herkimer Road. *Courtesy Oneida County Historical Society*

Below: Mappa Hall, Barneveld, 1930s.
Courtesy Oneida County Historical Society

CHAPTER EIGHT

Sports, Nature Provide Recreation

The day-to-day grind of working in the area's numerous mills and factories offered little relaxation for area residents. Luckily, the Mohawk Valley Region was dotted with a number of lakes and parks that were welcome distractions for local inhabitants.

Area parks and lakes, like Summit Park, located in Oriskany, and Sylvan Beach, provided many with a day in the sun complete with canoeing, swimming and fishing.

Dance clubs and pavilions were also very popular in the area and were home to many local bands and orchestras.

Community activities, such as bicycle clubs, choir groups,and other such organizations, often held events throughout the region that attracted many visitors.

Local theatres like Stanley, the Olympic and the James, were a haven for motion pictures, plays and local performances like the Haydn Male Chorus.

Of course, sports were very prevalent in the area Local high school teams from Utica, Rome and neighboring communities battled against one another in basketball, baseball, football, and many other games.

While some non-tradition forms of recreation– like airplane shows and gun clubs did exist– music, sports and nature were the most often the choices for entertainment in the Mohawk Valley Region.

Left: Cycle club members, Utica, 1888. *Courtesy Oneida County Historical Society*

Right: Hamilton College basketball team, Clinton, 1902. *Courtesy Oneida County Historical Society*

Left: Frankfort Citizen Drum Corp, late 1800s. *Courtesy Oneida County Historical Society*

Below: Trenton I.O.O.F. Band at the Boonville Fair, September 5, 1894. In the photo: D.J. Jones, E.B. Worden, W.E. Terrell, Herb Griffith, C.A. French, F.L. Worden, J.G. Wells, Ed Cramer, C.B. Watkins, G.W. Jones, Fred Pfeifer, Ham Corner, Ed Blust, Jack Nester, J.E. Bosworth. *Courtesy Oneida County Historical Society*

Opposite page: St. Vincent's School For Boys basketball game, circa 1900. St. Vincent's vs. Lincoln. *Courtesy Oneida County Historical Society*

Above: Hamilton College track team, Clinton, 1901. *Courtesy Oneida County Historical Society*

Above, right: Sylvan Beach was a popular place to cool off in the summertime, circa 1905. *Courtesy Oneida County Historical Society*

Right: Bicyclists (unknown) on Broad Street between John and Genesee, Utica, circa 1900. *Courtesy Oneida County Historical Society*

Left: Dancing Pavilion, Summit Park, circa 1905. *Courtesy Oneida County Historical Society*

Below, left: Sam S. Shubert Theatre, Utica, circa, 1905. *Courtesy Oneida County Historical Society*

Below: Sylvan Beach, bath house and toboggan, circa, 1905. *Courtesy Oneida County Historical Society*

Left: Bathing beach and toboggan slide at Sylvan Beach, 1905. In the 1920s, as more and more people began to own cars, Sylvan Beach became the playground of central New York. *Courtesy Oneida County Historical Society*

Below, left: Cooling off at the Summit Park Lake near Utica, circa 1905. *Courtesy Oneida County Historical Society*

Below: Entrance to Utica Park, circa 1910. *Courtesy Oneida County Historical Society*

Above: Haydn Male Chorus, Elsteddfod winner, 1915. *Courtesy Oneida County Historical Society*

Right: Druggist Clambake, Utica, 1911. *Courtesy Oneida County Historical Society*

Below: A.O.H. (Ancient Order of Hibernians) ball team clambake, Clinton, September 15, 1912. *Courtesy Oneida County Historical Society*

Above Sylvan Beach, circa 1915. The man in the water is identified as Steve Paul. *Courtesy Oneida County Historical Society*

Above, right: Elizabeth Paul at Sylvan Beach, circa 1915. *Courtesy Oneida County Historical Society*

Right: Vern Vermilyea, winner of the "open car hill climb contest up Vickerman Hill in Mohawk, 1919. *Courtesy Oneida County Historical Society*

Above: The Rockies Athletic Club football team from Utica, 1925. *Courtesy Oneida County Historical Society*

Above, left: Henry F. Miller, poses with his 1919 Cadillac Victoria and the trophy he won in the "closed car hill climb contest," up Vickerman Hill in Mohawk, 1919. *Courtesy Oneida County Historical Society*

Left: Utica cricket club, circa 1920. *Courtesy Oneida County Historical Society*

Left: Utica Mutual girls bowling team, 1921. Top row: Miss Evans, Miss Peters, Miss Lewis, Mrs. Hughes, Miss Brenner, Miss Moss, Mrs. Wood, Miss Herbig, Miss Schofer, Miss Schaeffer. Bottom row: Miss Steele, Miss McGraw, Miss Otto, Miss Intermill, Miss Wasse, Miss Dietz, Miss Steele, Miss Hammeline, Miss Koncelman. *Courtesy Oneida County Historical Society*

Below, left: Members of the B Sharp Musical Club in 1932: Ladies heading the membership campaign of the Utica Community Concert Association are seated, left to right; Mrs. E. B. M. Wortman, Mrs. Bessie Stewart Bannigan, Mrs. Harold V. Owens, president; Mrs. William B. Crouse and Mrs. Leon Bishop. Standing are Mrs. Robert C. Kincaid, Miss Margaret Griffith, Mrs. George Crowell, Mrs. P. J. Donahoe, Miss Harriet Woodworth, Miss Helen Hale Brockway, Mrs. Earl B. Worden and Mrs. C. H. Baldwin. *Courtesy Oneida County Historical Society*

Below: Utica Free Academy basketball team and city champs, 1929. Standing: Coach Edkins, W. Bohner, E. Garland, L. Wendt, C. Ehresman, F. McCann. Seated: J. Cahill, T. Macksey, D. Snell, F. Rabice, G. Jones. Officers: Dick Snell, captain, Francis McCann, manager. *Courtesy Oneida County Historical Society*

Above: Group of people gather to watch a magician perform tricks on Columbia Street, Utica, circa 1932. *Courtesy Oneida County Historical Society*

Above: Whitesboro Central School cheer leaders, 1938. Left to right: Helen Bush, Ernest Johnson, Lucille La Shombe, Gerald Murphy, Virginia Jones, Jack Spink, Eleanor Hebard, Gerald Donohoe, Alice Callahan. *Courtesy Oneida County Historical Society*

Right: St. Francis de Sales High School basketball team, 1939. Left to right, standing: Robert McNally, manager; Leo Carr, Raymond Jones, Edward Cahill, Bernard Banningan, Thomas Casalett, Robert Kelly, Gerald Kearney, Robert Costello, Stephen Carey, Joseph Wameling, William Halpin and Edward Duffy, captain. Kneeling, Walter Booth, Donald Orr, Robert Stein, Maryrose Baechle, Eileen Dwyer and Marie Albright. *Courtesy Oneida County Historical Society*

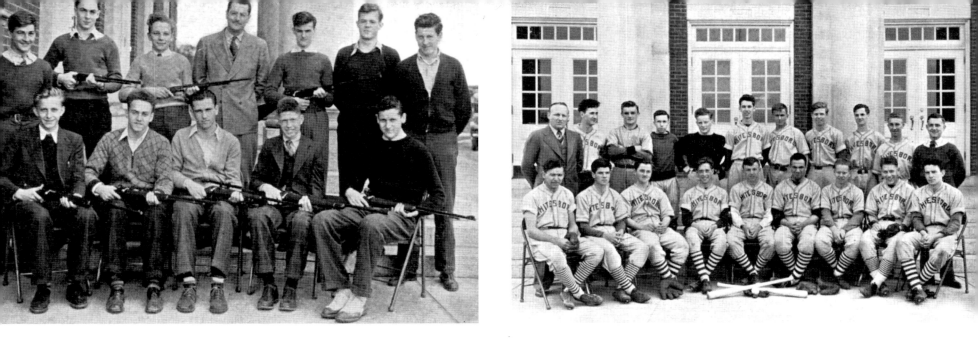

Above: Whitesboro Central School rifle club, 1938. Left to right, seated: Joseph Kosmider, Thomas Malsan, Keith Werthman, William Dumka, Lawrence Dedell. Standing: Melvin Humnicky, Theodore O'Connor, Kenneth Broadhurst, Mr. Buck, Thomas Carr, Fred Griffith, Richard Dedell. *Courtesy Oneida County Historical Society*

Above, right: Whitesboro Central School baseball team, 1938. Left to right, seated: Ernest Randall, Leonard Gifford, Julian Baranowski, Joseph Bialek, John Misiaszek, Louis Parent, Ernest Lathers, William Deming, John Cox. Standing: Mr. Frye, Melvin Brown, Donald Moore, William Rowlands, Thomas Cahill, Charles Emery, Edward Misiaszek, Donald Hensel, Howard Manor, Robert Kennerknecht, Frank Toper. *Courtesy Oneida County Historical Society*

Right: St. Francis de Sales High School baseball team, 1939. Left to right, standing: Louis Oliva, Edward Noonan, Robert Kelly, Joseph Wameling, Edward Kinney, Bernard Banningan, Edward Duffy, Jack McKennan, Robert McNally. Kneeling: Charles McCarthy, Dick Keating, Ray Fellito, David Greer, John Miller, Joseph Foley. *Courtesy Oneida County Historical Society*

CHAPTER NINE

Service a Part of Area's Heritage

From the very beginning of permanent settlements in the Mohawk Valley Region, there were fire and police departments, courthouses and buildings to house city, town and village offices.

Files of the Oneida County Historical Society are filled with photos of elected public officials, police officers, firefighters and court officials. There also are photos of some of the courthouses and judges who ran them.

The early photos of fire departments are fun to look at, with their horse-drawn vehicles speeding along cobblestone streets. There also is a photographic record of the change in the early 20th century from horse-drawn fire wagons to motorized fire trucks.

Many photos are available showing firehouses from the early years of the mid- 19th century to today's modern structures.

Early police photos also are fun to look at with the mustachioed gentlemen decked out in fancy uniform and helmet.

Most of the courthouses were architectural masteries and some of them are still standing—including the Oneida County courthouse on Elizabeth Street Utica and ones in places like Rome and Whitesboro.

Post offices have dotted the region from as early as the late 18th century and there are photos available of some of them.

Left: Utica Fire Department employees pose with engine No. 2 in front of the Central Fire Station on Elizabeth Street, 1915. *Courtesy Oneida County Historical Society*

Right: Combination wagon No. 8, Utica Fire Department, early 1900s. *Courtesy Oneida County Historical Society*

Above: Daniel Butterfield as a 31-year-old Brigadier General in the Civil War. *Courtesy Oneida County Historical Society*

Above, right and right: Oneida County Board of Supervisors meeting in Old John Street Courthouse, Utica, 1887. *Courtesy Oneida County Historical Society*

Above: Utica Police department, 1889. In the photo: Chas. Schaffer, Geo. Dressel, John Carrou, Geo. Berg, J.M. Griffith, John R. Bucher, Edward Quinn Assistant Chief, James Landers, H. Evans, John J. Coakley, James Evans, Fred Cheney, August Freidel, Chas. Devine, John Latham, John Barry, John P. Mason, Timothy Dillon, Jerry J. Lyons, Chas. F. Cleveland, Joseph Brunner, Peter R. Arheilger, Chas. Reed Captain, David Ross, John Scheiderman, Geo. Keating, Wm. Shorer, Geo. Soley, Chas. M. Dagwell, Chief. *Courtesy Oneida County Historical Society*

Left: Utica's Old City Hall on Genesee Street in 1890. *Courtesy Oneida County Historical Society*

Right: St. Elizabeth Hospital, Utica, early 1900s. *Courtesy Oneida County Historical Society*

Below, right: St. Luke's Home and Hospital, Utica, circa, 1905. *Courtesy Oneida County Historical Society*

Below: Rome City Hall, circa 1905. *Courtesy Oneida County Historical Society*

Above: Butler Memorial Hall, New Hartford, 1905. *Courtesy Oneida County Historical Society*

Right: Members of the Utica Fire Department demonstrate their new ladder truck No. 2 at the corner of Cooper and Cornelia streets, circa 1905. *Courtesy Oneida County Historical Society*

Below: Faxton Hospital in 1908. *Courtesy Oneida County Historical Society*

Above: President William Howard Taft and Vice-President James S. Sherman pose with the reception committee in Utica, 1908. *Courtesy Oneida County Historical Society*

Right: James S. Sherman speaking at his home on Genesee Street in 1908 when notified he was the U.S. Vice President nominee. *Courtesy Oneida County Historical Society*

Below: Utica Fire Department members, 1910. *Courtesy Oneida County Historical Society*

Above: United States Post Office, Utica, 1909. In the photo: Hon. J.S. Sherman, Harry W. Roberts, P.M., W.M. Philleo, L.A. Jones, S.P. Pugh, C.H. Smith, Geo. Firsching, F.J. M. Dicks, R.J. Ryan, L.E. Jones, F.R. Groves, W.R. Boyle, J.S. Roth, F.L. Kellogg, N.W. Leibel, E. Heinrich, J.E. Thomas, C.W. Jones, H.M. Jones, F.W. Owston, E.S. O'Connor, E.D. Freytag, W.H. Griffin, N.J. Scheiderich, J.H. Pinkstone, F.H. Fullride, W.G. W. Seiler, E.F. Leonard, R.W. Jones, T.A. Bogan, A.F. Rockwell, J.F. Teesdale, W.I. Everson, E.H. Snyder, H.R. Jones, B.A. Sherman, Roy Cunningham, B.L. Ambrose, A.F. Bockmann, C.F. Brodt, V.P. Raymond, C.E. Whitcher, M.J. Kavanagh, C.D. Gray, P.J.Lynch, H.A. Ulrich, E.T. Vaughn, O.N. Bartley, D.F. White, E.D. Fox, J.A. Dining, A.S. Thayer, J.E. McAvoy, A.C. Darrigrand, Earl Edwards, W.G. Kingsley, N.L. Clarke, J.B. Frick, E.L. Perry, W.J. Russell, A.P. Jewett, M.T. Pittman, C.J. Ulrich, J. Stiefvater, F.G. Hammond, A.N. Dougherty, A.J. Ryan, J.C. Roboy, F.J. Hamlin, Chas. Walker, F.M. Clark, J.J. Adams, D. Daniele, M. James, T.C. Fisher, Edw. Bedford, J.F. Lanning, C.T. Miller, A.L. Murcodk, Jr., H.B. Dye, W.L. Hinton, R.E. McCreary, F.J. Wendt, J.W. Williams, W.W. Hurlburt, J.F. Rice, F.S. Schindler, L.W. Snell, O.R. Aikenbrecker, W.H. Rowland, F.P. Mowers, J.F. Murray, G.R. Kellogg, W.E. Fisher, C.B. Greeker, G.F. Smith, J.T. Williams, C.E. Wiegand, C.F. Leary, J.S. Carpenter, C.F. Robards, M.H. La Rouche, J.F. Brand, J.J. Cummings, O.D. Jones, J.R. Morris, W.J. Rickard, J.S. Clark, P.J. Marion, A.G. Richards, J.J. Horrigan, H.A. Zoeckler, H. Zockler, M.B. Farrell. *Courtesy Oneida County Historical Society*

Right: Utica Fire Department chemical engine No. 2 (formerly No. 3), Central Avenue station on Elizabeth Street, 1915. *Courtesy Oneida County Historical Society*

Above: Utica Fire Department employees pose with the American La France truck No. 2 in front of the Central fire station on Elizabeth Street, 1915. *Courtesy Oneida County Historical Society*

Right: Utica Fire Department chief's cutter in front of the Central Fire Station on Elizabeth Street, 1915. *Courtesy Oneida County Historical Society*

Left: 17th contingent of Rome, NY, US Army, enroute for Camp Wheeler in Macon, GA, October 23, 1918. *Courtesy Rome Historical Society*

Below, left: New Hartford Volunteer Fire Department running team poses outside fire house in New Hartford on Park Street, circa 1915. *Courtesy Oneida County Historical Society*

Below: Utica City Hall Tower used as a bulletin board during World War I to track local employers participation in Liberty Loans, circa 1917. *Courtesy Oneida County Historical Society*

Above: Sherrill fire department, circa 1925. *Courtesy Oneida County Historical Society*

Opposite page: Utica fire men, 1920. Left to right: Sgt. P. Dressell, J. Steph, Wm. Zoller, unidentified, unidentified, Ben Lent, Leo Miller, Sr., Tom Gleason, Tom Holligan, Jack Nesius, Joe Leddy, Ed Gallagher, Frank Jennings, Tim Kinney, Leo Miller, Jr., Pete Knopka. *Courtesy Oneida County Historical Society*

Above, left: The Utica Fire Department's Deputy Chiefs in 1934, were, from left; Joseph McIncrow, Charles Keefe, William McGauley, John Darby and James Donovan. *Courtesy Oneida County Historical Society*

Below, left: Pumpers being tested at the Foamite-Childs Factory pond, Utica, circa 1925. *Courtesy Oneida County Historical Society*

Below: General Hospital, Utica, 1934. *Courtesy Oneida County Historical Society*

CHAPTER TEN

Tragedy Visits Mohawk Valley

Since the first settlers arrived in the Mohawk Valley Region in the mid-1780s, snowstorms have taken their toll in damaging homes, farms and the geographical landscape.

The history of the region is dotted with stories of people losing their lives in fierce blizzards.

Winter snow, however, was not the only catastrophe that plagued the region. Floods swept through areas of Oneida County, like the small settlement of Oriskany Falls that ravaged local residents' homes and businesses.

Fire also wreaked havoc in and around the county, particularly in Utica where infernos often devoured many prominent establishments. One of which was Genesee Flats that burned in 1896.

The large building located on Genesee Street was the first apartment house of its kind in the city. After the fire, a new Olbiston apartment building was built on the site.

There were other disastrous fires, too, such as the YMCA fire at the southwest corner of Bleecker and Charlotte streets in March 1907. The blaze destroyed the building and forced the facility to move to a new location on Washington street.

Left: Ruins of the Great Fire in Utica, March 1884. The fire burned most of the block bounded by the east side of Genesee Street., Catherine Street and Charlotte Street and the present Oriskany Street. *Courtesy Oneida County Historical Society*

Right: Ruins of Genesee Flats, the first Utica apartment house built in 1892 and destroyed by fire, 1896. Four lives were lost in this fire. *Courtesy Oneida County Historical Society*

Left and Below: Great fire in Utica, March 2, 1884.
Courtesy Oneida County Historical Society

Above, left and right, following page: Fraser's fire, May 10, 1905. Word spread through the town about dinnertime that Fraser's was on fire. In a matter of minutes, the building was emptied of clerks and office staff. Every company of the fire department was on the scene in record time. It looked for a time as though the whole block of businesses would go up in flames. As it was, damage to the stores adjacent to Fraser's was considerable. In the Genesee Street block, from the left, were the A.B. Mather Bank, at Genesee and Bleecker. Tygert's Restaruant, John H. Sheehan's Drug Store, John A. Roberts Drygoods Store, Buckingham & Moak, Piano Dealers with Mansbach's Millinery Store on the first floor. Fraser's Drygoods Store, Howarth & Ballard's Drug Store, the Parlor Shoe Store and Parker's Grocery at Genesee and Elizabeth steets. John G. Swan, office manager for Fraser's store then, recalls how Robert Fraser dispatched his store buyers to New York the day after the fire for an entire new stock of everything from thread to carpets. Within 30 days Fraser's had its headquarters established in the Sherwood & Golden crockery store at 125 Genesee. Shortly thereafter Robert Fraser bought that store, crockery and all, and did a flourishing business there while the burned-out drygoods store was being rebuilt. *Courtesy Oneida County Historical Society*

Above: Ice Storm, Utica, February 15, 1909. *Courtesy Oneida County Historical Society*

Above, left and left: Aftermath of the YMCA fire, 100 block of Bleecker Street on the southwest corner of Charlotte Street, Utica, March 1, 1907. *Courtesy Oneida County*

Above: Aftermath of an ice and sleet storm on February 15, 1909 on Whitesboro Street in West Utica. Ice storms presented a serious problem for trolley lines, as falling tree branches tore down power wires. *Courtesy Oneida County Historical Society*

Above, right: Flood water during the 1910 flood in Herkimer. *Courtesy Oneida County Historical Society*

Right: Homeowner came back to retrieve a few treasure's after her home was destroyed by the 1910 flood in Herkimer. *Courtesy Oneida County Historical Society*

Left: Clearing the track after the 1910 flood in Herkimer. *Courtesy Oneida County Historical Society*

Below Left: Ruins near the round house in Herkimer during the 1910 flood. *Courtesy Oneida County Historical Society*

Below: Re-opening Albany Street in Herkimer after the Great Flood in Herkimer in 1910. *Courtesy Oneida County Historical Society*

Above: A 75-car train sits derailed on the New York Central tracks in Stanwix, east of Rome on April 8, 1910. None of the passengers was injured on the freight and passenger train, but one fireman was killed. *Courtesy Oneida County Historical Society*

Left: A train wreck on the New York Central tracks between Rome and Oriskany, April 8, 1910. *Courtesy Oneida County Historical Society*

Opposite page: Herkimer flood in March of 1910. Photo shows scene on Mohawk Street in village of Herkimer. *Courtesy Oneida County Historical Society*

Below: Mountains of ice left by the Herkimer flood near the coal sheds, 1910. *Courtesy Oneida County Historical Society*

Above: Debris carried by flood waters during the June 11, 1917 flood, Oriskany Falls. *Courtesy Oneida County Historical Society*

Right: Feed Mill after the flood swept through Oriskany Falls, June 11, 1917. *Courtesy Oneida County Historical Society*

Above: Damage left by the June 11, 1917 flood, Oriskany Falls. *Courtesy Oneida County Historical Society*

Above, right: Flood in Oriskany Falls June 11, 1917 along the lower Waterville Street. *Courtesy Oneida County Historical Society*

Below Right: Gardner Building fire at Genesee and Columbia Street in downtown Utica, February, 1, 1947. *Courtesy Oneida County Historical Society*

Below: Utica Free Academy fire. *Courtesy Oneida County Historical Society*

CHAPTER ELEVEN

Everyone Loves A Parade

Cheerful public demonstrations in the Mohawk Valley Region were always marked with spectacle during the 19th and early 20th century.

Citizens of Oneida County and elsewhere in the region participated in a number of national movements and did so through parades, marches and celebrations. One example was at the Independence Day Parade in 1900 where a large group of women marched down Genesee Street in Utica in support of woman's suffrage.

Not all celebrations in the area were for political matters. Local residents organized parades to celebrate the commencement of regional firemen's convention, graduation or to commemorate the return of a local hero.

The parades that honored those who served in war were most impressive

and involved the participation of countless marching bands, fraternal order regiments and company floats.

Also, the parades and celebrations of the time were numerous in number due to the area's high degree of optimism from fast growing businesses, popular new establishments and a mounting sense of local pride.

Left: Welcome Home Parade in Utica following World War I. *Courtesy Oneida County Historical Society*

Right: Trenton Citizen's Band and Newport Fire Company at Newport, September 5, 1895. *Courtesy Oneida County Historical Society*

Above: Conkling Unconditionals, a Republican marching club of Utica, marching up Genesee Street, Utica, 1904. *Courtesy Oneida County Historical Society*

Above Left: Odd Fellows Parade at the corner of Oriskany and Genesee, Utica, 1890. Photo taken from Devereux Building window. *Courtesy Oneida County Historical Society*

Left: Vote for women suffragette parade, Utica, July 4, 1900. *Courtesy Oneida County Historical Society*

Above: It's "Notification Day" in Utica August 18, 1908 when James Sherman is told officially he is U.S. vice-presidential candidate. The motorcade is on Genesee-Elizabeth-Columbia intersection on way to Sherman's House. *Courtesy Oneida County Historical Society*

Above, left: G.A.R. 41st Annual Encampment, Utica, June 18, 1907. *Courtesy Oneida County Historical Society*

Below, left: The Conkling Unconditional Marching Band on Notification Day in July 1908. James Schoolcraft Sherman is notified he is Republican candidate for U.S. vice-president. The parade is marching south along Genesee Street in Utica. *Courtesy Oneida County Historical Society*

Below: Parade in Whitesboro, circa 1912. Float represents Wind's Bakery of Whitesboro. Man standing is Wybo Wind, founder of Wind's Bakery. *Courtesy Oneida County Historical Society*

Left: Oneida County Firemen's Convention, third annual automobile club hill climb at Oriskany Falls, July 3-4, 1915. The Oriskany Falls Fire Department is going through one of their stunts in the photograph. *Courtesy Oneida County Historical Society*

Below, left: Oneida County Firemen's Convention parade in Village Square, July 3-4, 1915. *Courtesy Oneida County Historical Society*

Below: Welcome Home Parade, World War I, Utica. *Courtesy Oneida County Historical Society*

Left: A "Welcome Home" arch hangs over Genesee Street in Utica to welcome World War I vets back from the war in 1919. The view is north along Genesee Street, with the Old City Hall to the far left, and the Radisson Hotel now sits where Puritan Men's Clothing once sat. *Courtesy Oneida County Historical Society*

Below, left: Welcome Home parade in Utica following World War I. The banner carried by members of the YWCA says: "The Girls Behind the Men Behind The Guns." *Courtesy Oneida County Historical Society*

Below: Welcome Home parade in Utica following World War I. Members of the Red Cross can be seen in this photo. *Courtesy Oneida County Historical Society*

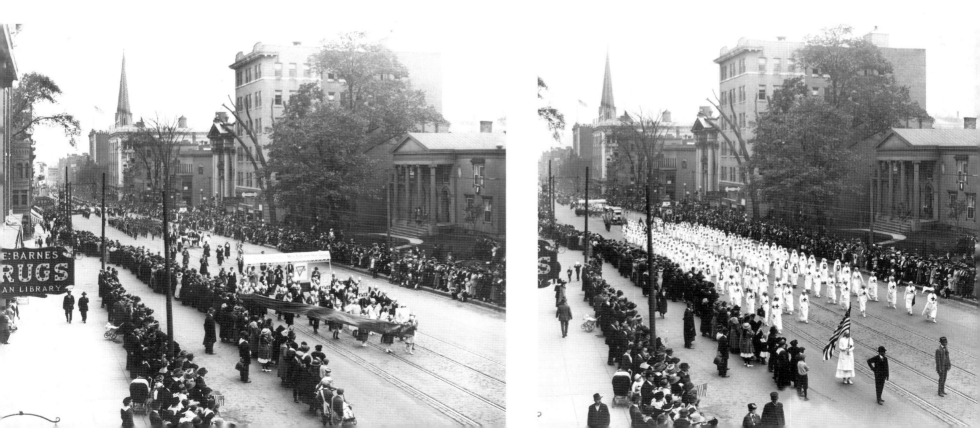

Left: Utica Baby Parade, on the grounds of Utica Free Academy, circa 1920. *Courtesy Oneida County Historical Society*

Below, left and right: A 1919 Victory Parade for returning World War I veterans in Herkimer. *Courtesy Herkimer Historical Society*

Opposite page: Otis Motor Sales Company and Utica Motor Car company celebrating Peace Day, November 11, 1918. *Courtesy Oneida County Historical Society*

All Photos this Page: Utica Centennial Celebration parade. *Courtesy Oneida County Historical Society*

Above and Left: Utica Centennial Celebration activities. *Courtesy Oneida County Historical Society*